THE BEST BOOK OF

Snakes

Christiane Gunzi

KINGFISHER

BOSTON

Contents

Created for Kingfisher by
Picthall & Gunzi Limited

Author and editor: Christiane Gunzi
Designer: Dominic Zwemmer
Illustrator: Michael Langham Rowe
Additional illustrations: Ian Jackson,
 David Marshall, Phil Weare, David Wright
Consultant: Mark O'Shea

First published in 2003
10 9 8 7 6 5 4 3 2 1

ISBC/0604/WKT/MA(MA)/128KMA/C

Copyright © Kingfisher
Publications 2003

LIBRARY OF CONGRESS CATALOGING-IN-PUBLICATION DATA
Gunzi, Christiane.
    The best book of snakes/Christiane Gunzi.
      p. cm.
    Summary: Introduces snakes of the world,
  including the cobra, anaconda, and various
  constrictors and sea snakes.
  1. Snakes—Juvenile literature. [1. Snakes.] I. Title.

QL666.O6G86 2003
597.96—dc21

2003044653

ISBN 0-7534-5837-3

Printed in China

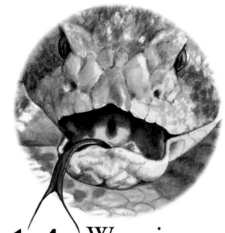

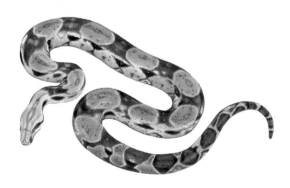

Meet the snake

Eye with no eyelids

Forked tongue

Special "pit" that can sense heat

Nostril

Long, hinged fangs

Two rows of teeth in roof of mouth

Two rows of teeth in bottom jaw

Pit viper

Snakes are amazing animals. They have no legs but can crawl, swim, and climb well. All snakes hunt their prey, and they always swallow it whole. Some snakes, such as vipers, use venom (poison) to kill their prey, while pythons squeeze their victims to death. All snakes are covered in scaly skin, and they molt (shed their skin) several times each year. Several species are very venomous and extremely dangerous. But most snakes are completely harmless!

A snake's body

A snake is covered with scales. Its forked tongue flicks in and out to pick up smells in the air. Some snakes, such as this viper, have "pits" on their faces to help them find warm-blooded prey.

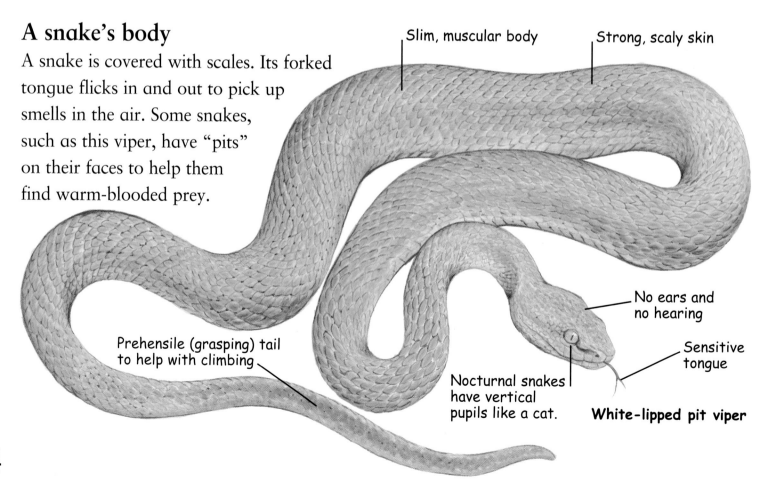

Slim, muscular body

Strong, scaly skin

No ears and no hearing

Sensitive tongue

Nocturnal snakes have vertical pupils like a cat.

Prehensile (grasping) tail to help with climbing

White-lipped pit viper

4

Power of the python

The reticulated python is a powerful predator. It is not venomous, but it is so strong that it can overpower and eat large mammals. During the day this handsome snake likes to bask in trees in the sun.

A leopard is a predator, but it can also be prey for a python.

A world of snakes

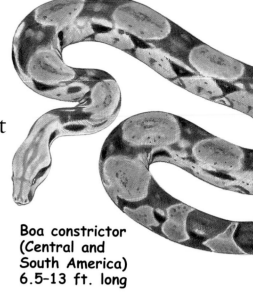

**Boa constrictor
(Central and
South America)
6.5–13 ft. long**

Snakes have existed for millions of years. There are about 2,800 different types, and most are harmless. Snakes belong to several groups such as the python, cobra, and viper families. These cold-blooded animals are reptiles, so they need the heat of the sun to keep them warm. Most snakes live in the warmest parts of the world. The world's most venomous snakes are found in Africa and Australia.

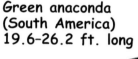

**Asian sunbeam snake
(Southeast Asia)
3.3–4.3 ft. long**

**Green anaconda
(South America)
19.6–26.2 ft. long**

**Western coral snake
(U.S. and Mexico)
16–22 in. long**

Champion constrictors

The green anaconda is the largest and heaviest snake, and the reticulated python is the longest. Both of these beautifully patterned creatures live in the tropics, close to water. They are both "constrictors," so they kill their prey by squeezing it until it suffocates.

**Brahminy blind snake
(Worldwide)
6–7 in. long**

**Gaboon viper
(Africa)
3.9–6.5 ft. long**

**Reticulated python
(Southeast Asia)
19.6–32.7 ft. long**

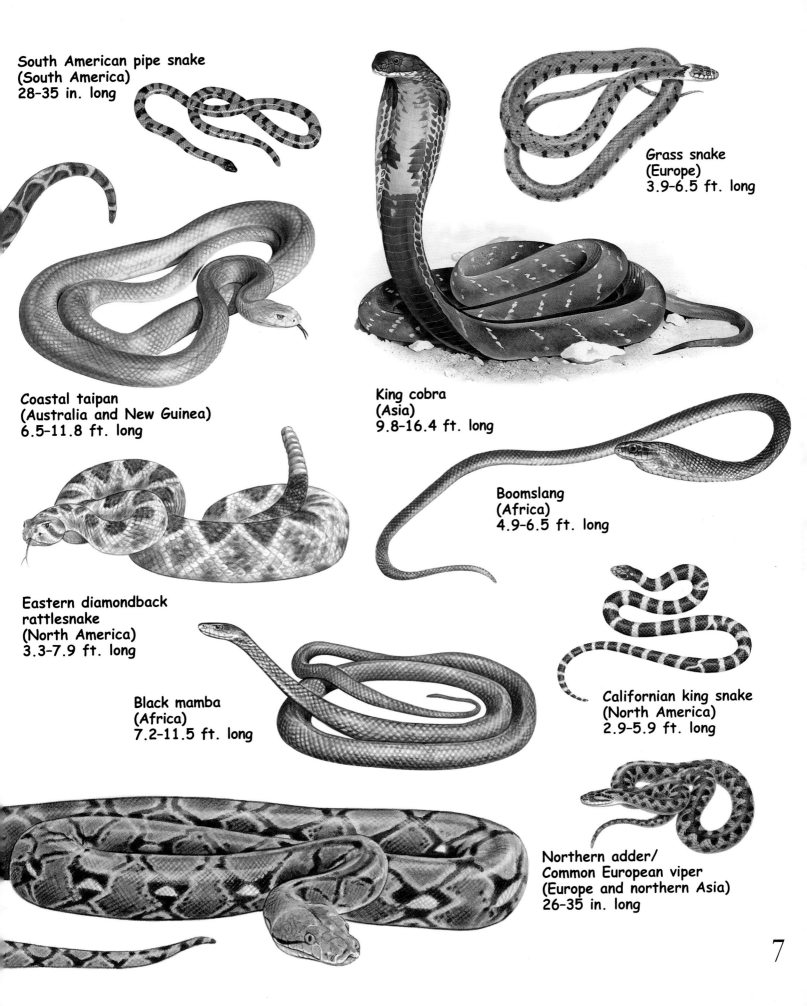

South American pipe snake
(South America)
28–35 in. long

Grass snake
(Europe)
3.9–6.5 ft. long

Coastal taipan
(Australia and New Guinea)
6.5–11.8 ft. long

King cobra
(Asia)
9.8–16.4 ft. long

Boomslang
(Africa)
4.9–6.5 ft. long

Eastern diamondback
rattlesnake
(North America)
3.3–7.9 ft. long

Black mamba
(Africa)
7.2–11.5 ft. long

Californian king snake
(North America)
2.9–5.9 ft. long

Northern adder/
Common European viper
(Europe and northern Asia)
26–35 in. long

7

Sidewinding over the sand

When a desert snake has to travel over loose, hot sand, it keeps most of its belly off the ground by throwing its body forward in a series of loops. Only a small part of the snake's body touches the ground at a time. This movement is called sidewinding, and snakes that do this are known as sidewinders.

Sidewinding adder in the Namib desert

Eyes are on top of the head so the adder can see prey when the rest of its body is hidden in the sand.

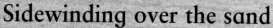

8

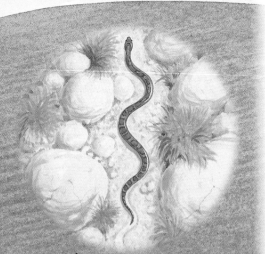

Corn snake

Serpentining snakes

Long, slim snakes move their bodies in a series of "S"-shaped curves while they push against little bumps on the ground.

Anaconda

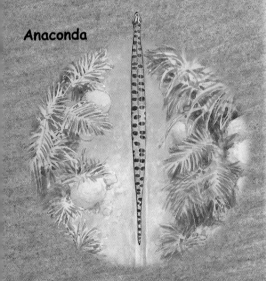

Caterpillar crawling

Big, heavy snakes, such as pythons and boas, creep along in a straight line like a caterpillar. Snakes use special scales on their bellies to grip the ground.

How snakes move

Snakes move in several different ways. The most common is a method called serpentining.

There are powerful muscles inside a snake's body. These muscles produce a series of waves that travel along the snake's body, from its head to its tail. Some snakes, such as black mambas, can move very fast in short bursts. But most snakes do not move quickly unless they are being threatened.

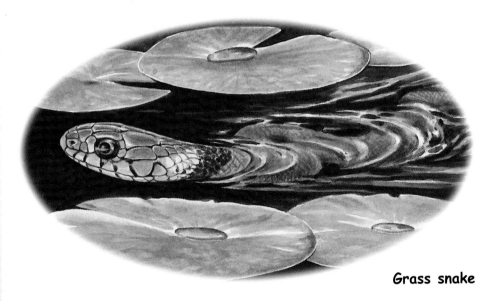

Grass snake

Taking a dip

A grass snake often swims in rivers with its head out of the water, searching for frogs and fish. These reptiles move well on land and are also found in forests and marshes. Grass snakes are completely harmless to humans. If one is caught, it usually pretends to be dead!

9

Baby snakes

Some snakes, such as vipers and boas, give birth to live young. Others, such as cobras and pythons, lay eggs. Snakes that give birth to live young have the most babies. Egg-laying snakes like to lay their eggs in warm, damp places. Unlike the hard shells of bird and turtle eggs, snake eggs are leathery. Once the young are born or hatch from their eggs they are left on their own by their mother.

Rattlesnake males wrestling for a mate

Snake wrestling

Some male snakes have a wrestling match to decide which one will mate with the female. They lift up the front of their bodies and push each other around!

Carpet python and eggs

Shaking snake

A female carpet python lays 12–54 eggs. Unlike other egg-laying snakes, which lay their eggs and then abandon them, pythons coil around the eggs to keep them warm. The mother snake trembles from time to time, and this may help her eggs develop.

Royal (or ball) python hatching from its egg

Hatching out

A baby snake cuts its way out of its shell using a sharp "egg tooth" at the front of its mouth. The egg collapses once the snake has hatched.

10

Stunning stripes

The San Francisco garter snake is one of the most attractive snakes in the world. During the summer female garter snakes give birth to 12–50 live young. This snake lives close to water in meadows, marshes, and damp forests in California. It is an endangered species because its natural habitat is under threat.

San Francisco garter snake with newborn young

Hunting and feeding

Snakes are carnivores—this means that they eat other animals. Some snakes kill their prey with venom, so they are known as venomous. Others kill their prey by squeezing, or constricting, it—these are called constrictors. All snakes have special lower jaws that can expand, making their mouths open very wide. This means that snakes can eat animals that are much larger than they are!

Copperhead

Fierce fangs
Venomous snakes inject prey with poisonous venom through sharp, pointed teeth called fangs. The venom kills the prey very quickly.

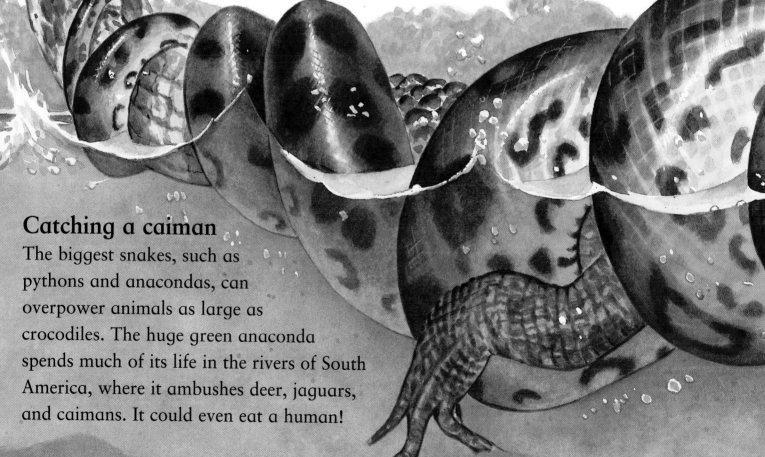

Catching a caiman
The biggest snakes, such as pythons and anacondas, can overpower animals as large as crocodiles. The huge green anaconda spends much of its life in the rivers of South America, where it ambushes deer, jaguars, and caimans. It could even eat a human!

A snake that swallows eggs

1 The toothless egg-eating snake eats birds' eggs. It holds the egg in place with its body and then swallows it.

2 As the snake swallows the egg lots of sharp "spurs" in its throat puncture the egg so that it breaks.

3 The contents of the egg go into the snake's stomach, and after a while the eggshell is regurgitated.

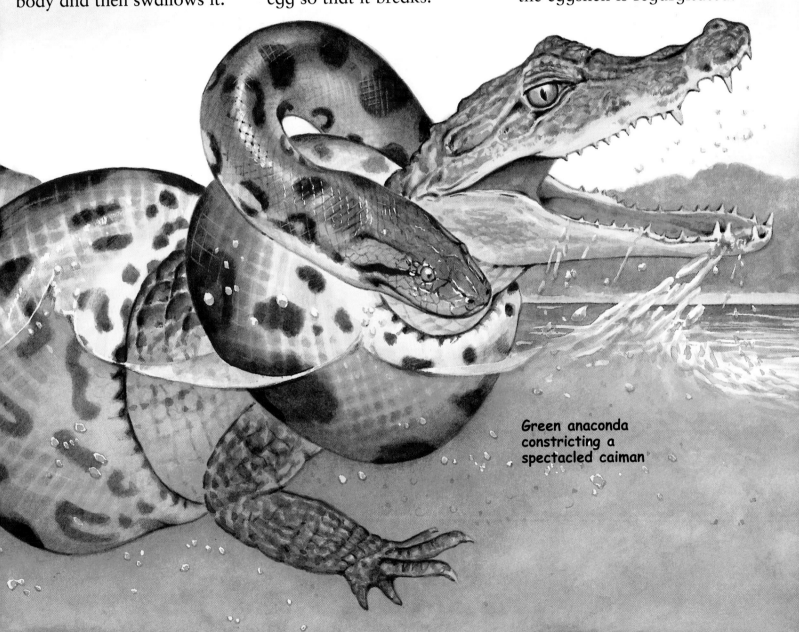

Green anaconda constricting a spectacled caiman

Warning signals

The venom from the fangs of a venomous snake is so deadly that many people are afraid of all snakes. But a snake only attacks when it is alarmed, hungry, or feels threatened. It will usually give a warning signal before it strikes. The snake may make a loud noise, lift its head up, or inflate its body to make itself look bigger. All of these signals tell its enemies to stay far away!

Angry cobra

When a cobra is annoyed, it lifts up the front of its body and spreads out its "neck hood." If this warning is ignored, the snake may attack.

A rattlesnake lifts up its tail and shakes the "rattle" loudly.

Huffing and puffing

The puff adder is very dangerous. It is so well camouflaged that it is difficult to see. When a puff adder is disturbed, it puffs out its body, hisses loudly, and then strikes. Its venom can kill a rat in seconds.

14

Deadly striker

When a western diamondback rattlesnake is alarmed, it lifts up the front of its body into an "S" shape and rattles its tail. This warns others to leave it alone. When the snake strikes, it is very quick, and its bite can kill a human.

West African gaboon viper in a pile of leaves

Lethal in the leaves

The gaboon viper is so perfectly disguised that it is almost impossible to see it among the leaves on the forest floor. It hunts by waiting for rats, squirrels, and other prey to scurry past. Even the top of this snake's head looks like a dead leaf!

Color and camouflage

Snakes have a perfect way of hiding from prey and predators. The different colors and patterns on a snake's body help disguise it— this is known as camouflage. Desert snakes are the color of sand, and forest snakes may be patterned like leaves so that predators and prey do not see them among the trees. Some snakes, such as coral snakes, have bright bands of color that warn enemies to stay away.

Like a twig
The brown vine snake is the same shape as the long, thin vines that grow up trees in the forests where it lives. When this snake stays still, it is very difficult to see.

Friend or foe?
Some harmless snakes look like venomous snakes. The colors and patterns on a milk snake, or false coral snake, are very similar to those on a deadly coral snake. It is important to learn the difference!

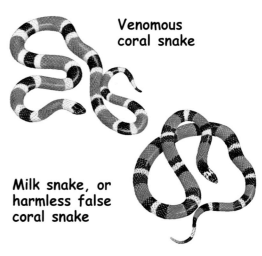

Venomous coral snake

Milk snake, or harmless false coral snake

King cobra

The world's longest venomous snake is the king cobra. This is the only snake that builds nests. The female pulls dead leaves into a mound with her body and then makes two underground "rooms" in it. One room is for her, and the other is for her eggs. She lays up to 50 eggs and guards them fiercely. King cobras are extremely venomous, so a female protecting her eggs is very dangerous—even to elephants. She could kill an elephant with one bite on the tip of its trunk!

Female king cobra
fiercely guarding
her nest

Guarding the nest

If a king cobra feels threatened by another
animal, it growls deeply and shows one of
its fangs. It raises the front of its body off
the ground and flattens its neck hood, which
makes it look bigger. This behavior warns
animals to stay away or risk being bitten.

Swamp killer

This big, heavy snake is a type of pit viper and has a very venomous bite. The cottonmouth spends much of its life in water and lives in the swamps, rivers, and marshes of the United States. It is so named because the inside of its mouth is as white as pure cotton. The cottonmouth is not usually aggressive, but when this snake is annoyed, it opens its mouth wide to show its deadly fangs and the pure white lining of its mouth.

A cunning way to catch prey

Cottonmouths are born with bright yellow tails. These newborn snakes have an unusual way of catching the frogs that are their prey—they simply wave the tips of their tails. The frogs mistake the tails for wriggling worms and then get eaten!

20

White bite

During the day a cottonmouth basks in
the sun on logs and stones at the water's
edge. At dawn and dusk it hunts for fish,
frogs, lizards, turtles, birds, and other
snakes as well. The cottonmouth's
only real enemies are king snakes,
herons, and humans, of course!

**Cottonmouth striking
at a green frog**

21

Fast and furious

The black mamba is the longest venomous snake in Africa. Its bite is so deadly that its victims die within one hour of being bitten. Just two drops of venom from this snake's fangs are enough to kill a human. Mambas feed mostly on rodents such as rats. Like other snakes, they can open their mouths very wide and are able to swallow extremely large prey. The black mamba's closest relatives are green mambas. These beautiful snakes are deadly, too!

Green mamba

This green mamba spends its life in the trees of forests close to the East African coast. Its color camouflages it so well that other animals do not see the snake in the trees.

The only part of a black mamba that is black is the inside of its mouth.

Menacing mamba

This strong snake can speed along at 14 mph (23 km/h) over short distances. It is very good at climbing, too. A mamba can lift up the front of its body three feet (1m) off the ground to strike at prey such as rats.

Rats are a black mamba's favorite prey.

Ocean swimmers

Some snakes spend their entire lives in the sea, and they can stay underwater for hours at a time. These sea snakes have unusual paddle-shaped tails that help them swim. Like other snakes they shed their skin as they grow. But a sea snake does this more often, possibly to get rid of tiny creatures called parasites on its body. The beaked sea snake is one of the most venomous animals in the world. One bite contains enough venom to kill 50 people!

A sea snake's cousin

Sea kraits are closely related to sea snakes, but they come on land to lay their eggs. A true sea snake never goes on land and has live young.

Types of sea snakes

There are around 53 different species, or types, of sea snakes. Most live in oceans and on coral reefs. A few types of sea snakes are found in river estuaries and mangrove swamps.

Hardwickes' sea snake

Turtle-headed sea snake

Olive sea snake

Beaked, or common, sea snake

Horned sea snake

Trash builds up on the surface where the currents meet. The fish come here to eat, and the sea snakes eat the fish.

A sea snake's nostrils are high up on its head and have valves that open and close for swimming underwater.

Yellow-bellied sea snake

Far out at sea, in the middle of the Pacific Ocean, yellow-bellied sea snakes live in groups of thousands. During the day they feed close to the water's surface. They grab fish, such as mullet and anchovies, that shelter beneath their coils.

Graceful glider

In the lush rain forests of Southeast Asia there are flying snakes. These unusual creatures do not really fly, but they can glide through the air to escape from predators. If a flying snake needs to escape quickly from a bird of prey, it simply leaps into the air and glides safely to the ground. As the snake glides its ribs expand so that the underside of its body becomes wide and flat. This is a perfect shape for gliding. The most colorful of these snakes is the beautiful paradise tree snake.

A hawk overhead frightens a group of langur monkeys, and their noise scares the snake away.

Clever climber

The paradise tree snake is an excellent climber, and it can easily travel up the smooth bark of tall, straight trees. This slender snake has special ridges on the scales of its belly that help it grip as it climbs.

Living on the edge

The broad-headed snake lives under flat sandstone rocks on the edge of cliffs. It is one o the most endangered snakes in Australia. Most of this snake's natural habitat has been covered by the city of Sydney. Sadly there are no longer many places for this snake to live in the wild. Many people collect the sandstone under which it lives and put the rocks in their gardens!

Broad-headed snake in its natural habitat near Sydney, Australia

Snakes in danger

Like all wild animals snakes are threatened because their natural habitats, such as rain forests, are being destroyed. Snakes are also in danger from pollution in rivers and seas. But the biggest threat to snakes comes from humans. Every year thousands of snakes are rounded up and killed because people are afraid of them. If we do not protect these beautiful, fascinating animals in the wild, they may become extinct.

Chinese medicines

Snakeskin purse

How snakes are used

In some countries thousands of wild snakes are killed every year. Their beautiful skin is made into purses, shoes, wallets, and belts for tourists. In some parts of the world snakes are used in medicines, too.

Snakeskin shoes

Snakeskin belt

Road rage

In the desert areas of the world road surfaces become very hot in the sun. In the evenings desert snakes will often lie on these roads to warm themselves. Many snakes are accidently killed by traffic. Unfortunately some drivers will run over a snake on purpose, and many snakes are killed in this way.

Studying snakes

Snakes have existed for more than 65 million years, and there is still a lot to learn about these amazing animals. Scientists who study snakes are called herpetologists. They look at snakes in their natural habitats to discover exactly how they live. Like all animals snakes have a role to play in the natural world, and they deserve our respect. You can find out more about snakes by going to see them at a zoo or pet store.

Milking snakes

Experts collect venom from the fangs of venomous snakes. This is known as "milking." The venom is then made into "antivenin" to treat people who have been bitten by a venomous snake.

Seeing snakes close up

Reptile keepers often encourage visitors to look at snakes close up. If the keeper allows you to stroke a snake, you will discover that its skin is not slimy or cold but is dry and warm to touch!

Reptile keeper showing a python to some visitors

Glossary

camouflage The different colors and markings on a snake that help it hide in the wild.

carnivore An animal, such as a cat, dog, or snake, that eats meat.

cold-blooded An animal, such as a reptile, that must bask in the sun to warm its body. It cannot produce its own body heat.

constrictors Snakes, such as boas and pythons, that squeeze their victims to death.

egg tooth A temporary tooth that some baby snakes use to cut their way out of their shells.

extinct An animal or plant that has died out forever.

fangs The long, pointed teeth on a venomous snake that inject prey with venom.

habitat An animal's habitat is its natural home in the wild.

hood The part of a snake's neck that gets wider when the snake, such as a king cobra, feels threatened.

mammals Warm-blooded animals, such as deer, cats, and rats, that are covered with fur or hair, give birth to live young, and feed them milk.

molting Shedding the outer layer of skin. Snakes molt their skin every few weeks or months. The skin often comes off in one long piece.

nocturnal An animal that is active at night. Rat snakes are nocturnal animals.

parasites Tiny creatures that live inside or on another animal. Fleas and lice are parasites.

pits The tiny holes on some snakes' faces that help them sense prey.

predators Animals that hunt other animals. Snakes are predators.

prehensile tail A tail that can grasp. Some snakes that live in trees have prehensile tails for holding onto branches.

prey Animals that are hunted and eaten by snakes and other predators.

reptile Certain cold-blooded animals with scaly or leathery skin such as snakes, crocodiles, lizards, tortoises, and turtles.

species A group of animals that look alike and are very closely related to each other.

venom A poisonous liquid that venomous snakes inject into their prey when they bite it. Snakes also use venom for self-defense.

venomous Animals that use venom to kill prey. Sea snakes are highly venomous snakes.

warm-blooded An animal, such as a mammal or a bird, that produces its own body heat. These animals can live in cold places.

Index